SIDNEY CROSBY
NHL MVP AND CHAMPION

BY MAXWELL HAMMER

Published by The Child's World®
1980 Lookout Drive • Mankato, MN 56003-1705
800-599-READ • www.childsworld.com

ACKNOWLEDGMENTS
The Child's World®: Mary Berendes, Publishing Director
Red Line Editorial: Editorial direction
The Design Lab: Design
Amnet: Production
Design elements: Shutterstock Images
Photographs ©: Gene J. Puskar/AP Images, cover, 21; Paul Chiasson/AP Images, 5; Yearbook Library, 7; Adrian Wyld/AP Images, 9; Jonathan Hayward/AP Images, 11; Tom Hanson/AP Images, 13; Paul McKinnon/Shutterstock Images, 15; Matt Slocum/AP Images, 17; Keith Srakocic/AP Images, 19

Copyright © 2015 by The Child's World®
All rights reserved. No part of this book may be reproduced or utilized in any form or by any means without written permission from the publisher.

ISBN 9781631437403
LCCN 2014945310

Printed in the United States of America
Mankato, MN
November, 2014
PA02239

ABOUT THE AUTHOR
Maxwell Hammer grew up in the Adirondacks of New York before becoming an international sports reporter and children's book author. When not traveling the world on assignment, he spends his winters in Thunder Bay, Ontario, with his wife and pet beagle.

TABLE OF CONTENTS

CHAPTER 1 **SID THE KID** 4
CHAPTER 2 **YOUNG IN COLE HARBOUR** 6
CHAPTER 3 **"THE NEXT ONE"** 8
CHAPTER 4 **YOUNG PENGUIN** 10
CHAPTER 5 **BECOMING A STAR** 12
CHAPTER 6 **CAPTAIN CHAMPION** 14
CHAPTER 7 **OLYMPIC HERO** 16
CHAPTER 8 **WINTER CLASSIC DISASTER** 18
CHAPTER 9 **BACK IN BLACK** 20

FUN FACTS 22
GLOSSARY 23
TO LEARN MORE 24
INDEX 24

CHAPTER 1

SID THE KID

It was the 2014 Winter Olympics. Canada was the favorite to win the men's ice hockey tournament. Sidney Crosby was the team captain. The forward nicknamed "Sid the Kid" was one of the National Hockey League's (NHL's) biggest stars. He had won a Stanley Cup with the Pittsburgh Penguins. He had several scoring titles. But Crosby had also struggled with injuries in recent seasons. He failed to score in each of Canada's first five Olympic games.

Fans never lost faith. Crosby has a history of playing well in big games. And that's what he did in Canada's sixth game. Sweden was a tough opponent in the gold-medal game. But Crosby scored in the second period to put Canada up 2–0. It proved to be a turning point. Canada cruised to a 3–0 win. Crosby is considered one of the best playmakers of his generation. In this game, he showed why.

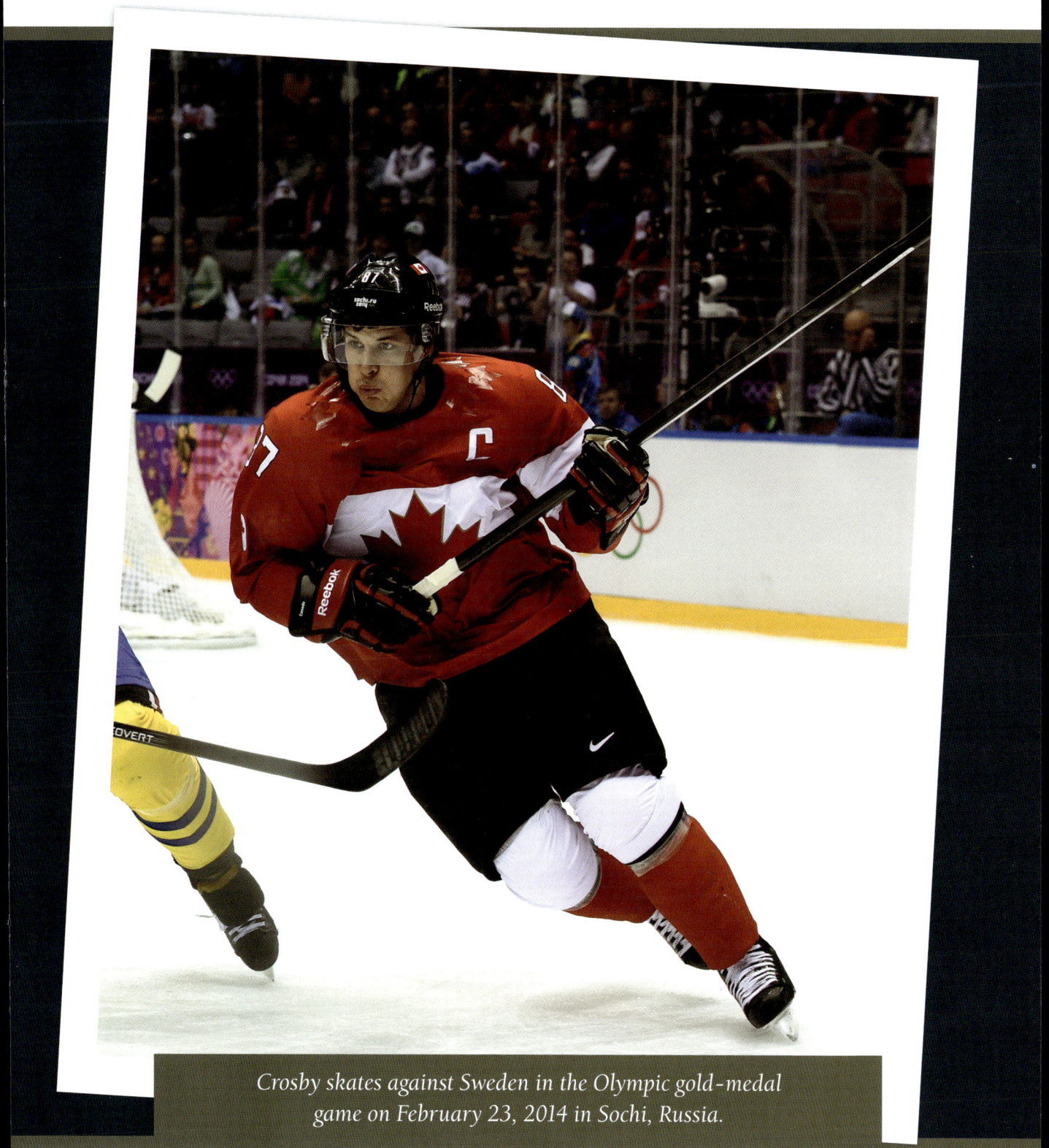

Crosby skates against Sweden in the Olympic gold-medal game on February 23, 2014 in Sochi, Russia.

CHAPTER 2

YOUNG IN COLE HARBOUR

Sidney grew up in a town called Cole Harbour. It is on the far eastern coast of Canada in Nova Scotia. Hockey is a big deal there. Sidney's dad was a star goalie. Sidney started skating at age three. He was quick and powerful on his skates. He had good instincts. Sidney was playing against older kids by age six.

Sidney moved to Minnesota in high school. He played for Shattuck-St. Mary's School. That school is known for its great hockey program. Jack Johnson, Matt Smaby, and Drew Stafford were Sidney's teammates there. All four players later went to the NHL. But Sidney was the star. He scored 72 goals and had 90 **assists** in 57 games that season. Meanwhile, the team won a national title.

> Crosby wears jersey number 87. In 2007 he signed a new **contract** for $8.7 million per season. Why? He was born on August 7, 1987 (or 8/7/87).

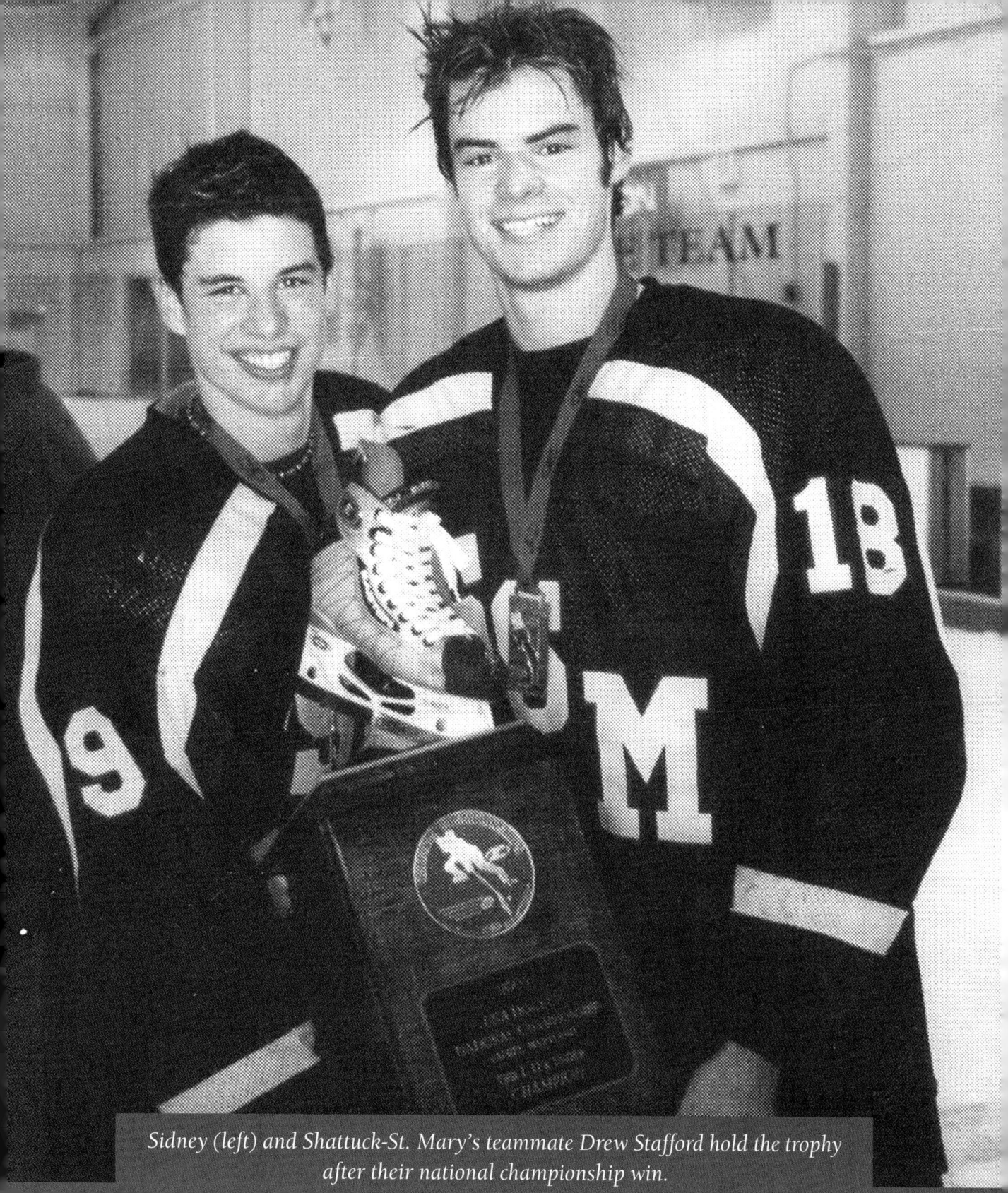
Sidney (left) and Shattuck-St. Mary's teammate Drew Stafford hold the trophy after their national championship win.

CHAPTER 3

"THE NEXT ONE"

Canadian hockey legend Wayne Gretzky was nicknamed "The Great One." Fans began calling Sidney "The Next One." Even Gretzky agreed. He said Crosby was the best young player he had seen since longtime Pittsburgh Penguins star Mario Lemieux.

Sidney left Shattuck St. Mary's after one year to play **junior hockey**. He decided to play in the Quebec Major Junior Hockey League (QMJHL). A team called Rimouski Océanic picked Sidney with the first overall pick in the league's **draft**. Most of the players in the QMJHL were 19 or 20 years old. But the 16-year-old Sidney was a star. He played 121 regular-season games over two years with the team. Sidney ended with 120 goals and 183 assists. The team was in last place before Sidney arrived in 2003. By 2005 they were league champions.

> Sidney twice played for Canada in the World Junior (Under-20) Championships. In 2005 he led his team past future Washington Capitals superstar Alex Ovechkin and Russia for the gold medal.

Crosby (right) keeps the puck away from an opponent during a Rimouski Océanic game against the Kelowna Rockets on May 25, 2005.

CHAPTER 4

YOUNG PENGUIN

The Pittsburgh Penguins picked Crosby with the first pick in the 2005 NHL Entry Draft. Crosby was just 18 years old during his **rookie** season in Pittsburgh. He had 39 goals and 63 assists. He was the youngest player to score more than 100 **points**. The team even named Crosby an alternate captain. Despite his stellar season, Crosby finished second in the voting for the NHL's Calder Memorial Trophy, awarded to the league's best rookie each year. The trophy went to Alex Ovechkin of the Washington Capitals.

> Crosby was still a teenager when he moved to Pittsburgh. So Penguins star Mario Lemieux invited Crosby to move in with him and his family. Crosby lived with Lemieux until 2010.

Crosby (left) stands with Pittsburgh Penguins owner and former star Mario Lemieux after the team took Crosby with the first pick of the 2005 NHL Draft.

CHAPTER 5

BECOMING A STAR

The Penguins had many talented young players. But 19-year-old Crosby was the brightest star. He scored 36 goals and had 84 assists in the 2006–07 season. His 120 points led the NHL. Both the NHL players and media voted for Crosby as the Most Valuable Player (MVP).

The Penguins returned to the playoffs. It was the first time since 2001. After the season, Crosby was named team captain. He was just 19 years and 297 days old. That made him the youngest NHL captain ever.

> At 19 Crosby became the youngest NHL scoring champion in 2006–07. Wayne Gretzky held the previous record. He was 20 when he scored 164 points in 1980–81.

Crosby (right) scores the game winner against the Ottawa Senators in the playoffs on April 14, 2007.

CHAPTER 6

CAPTAIN CHAMPION

Injuries forced Crosby to miss 21 games in 2007-08. The young captain came back strong. He led his team all the way to the Stanley Cup finals. But the Detroit Red Wings won the series in six games.

A Stanley Cup finals rematch in 2009 was even tighter. It all came down to Game 7 in Detroit. The game was intense. Then Crosby went down with an injury in the second period. But his teammates finished the job. Pittsburgh held on to win 2-1. Crosby, at age 21, became the youngest NHL captain to lift the Stanley Cup.

> Crosby had a memorable 22nd birthday. Each member of the Stanley Cup–winning team gets to spend one day with the trophy. Crosby brought the Cup to Cole Harbour on August 7, 2009. There was a huge celebration.

Cole Harbour, Nova Scotia, is proud of its homegrown NHL star.

CHAPTER 7

OLYMPIC HERO

The 2010 Winter Olympics were in Vancouver, Canada. Expectations for Crosby and Canada's men's hockey team were huge. Canada is a proud hockey country. The sport was invented there. Many of the best NHL players are Canadian.

Team Canada took a 2-0 lead over Team USA in the gold-medal game. But Team USA tied the game late. The two **rivals** went into overtime. Crosby clinched the gold medal when he slid the puck between U.S. goalie Ryan Miller's legs. Crosby leaped into the air and was mobbed by his teammates. He was a champion again, and this time it was for his country.

Crosby wears his gold medal during the men's ice hockey medal ceremony at the 2010 Winter Olympics in Vancouver, British Columbia.

CHAPTER 8

WINTER CLASSIC DISASTER

Crosby didn't have much time to celebrate after the 2010 Olympics. The NHL season started right back up. And the Penguins were looking to defend their Stanley Cup title. Crosby played a big role. His 51 goals led the NHL that season. However, the Montreal Canadiens beat Pittsburgh in the second round of the playoffs.

Still, Crosby was a huge star. He and Washington Capitals star Alex Ovechkin were rivals. The NHL decided to feature the two teams in the 2011 Winter Classic. That game is played outside in front of a huge crowd. Millions of people watch on TV. Crosby suffered

Crosby and the Penguins also played in the 2008 Winter Classic. He scored the game-winning goal in a shootout against the Buffalo Sabres.

a head injury during the game. He missed the final 41 games of the season and the playoffs. Then he played in only 22 games the next season. Some thought his career might be over.

Crosby falls to the ice after an injury during the Winter Classic on January 1, 2011, that would sideline him for the rest of the season.

CHAPTER 9

BACK IN BLACK

The Penguins never gave up on Crosby. They signed him to a new contract in 2012. It guaranteed he would play in Pittsburgh through 2024-25. A dispute between owners and players meant the 2012-13 season did not start until January. Finally, it did. And Crosby was ready. He led the Penguins to the conference finals. His fellow players again voted Crosby the MVP.

Crosby was finally healthy again in 2013-14. It showed. In February, he helped Canada win another Olympic gold medal. For the Penguins, his 68 assists and 104 points led the NHL. The team again fell short of its Stanley Cup goal, however. But with Crosby healthy and signed to a long-term deal, Penguins fans believe another championship is just a matter of time.

Crosby skates during a 4-3 win over the Tampa Bay Lightning on March 22, 2014.

FUN FACTS

SIDNEY CROSBY

BORN: August 7, 1987
HOMETOWN: Cole Harbour, Nova Scotia
TEAM: Pittsburgh Penguins (2005–)
POSITION: Center
HEIGHT: 5'11"
WEIGHT: 200 pounds
NHL DEBUT: October 5, 2005
STANLEY CUPS (WINS IN BOLD): 2008, **2009**
OLYMPIC WINTER GAMES
   (GOLD MEDALS IN BOLD): 2010, 2014
AWARDS
   Art Ross Trophy (NHL Leading Scorer): 2006–07, 2013–14
   Hart Memorial Trophy (MVP by Media): 2006–07
   Ted Lindsay Award (MVP by Players): 2006–07, 2012–13

GLOSSARY

assists (uh-SISTS) Assists are passes that lead directly to a goal. Crosby led the NHL with 75 assists in the 2013–14 season.

contract (KAHN-trakt) An agreement between a team and a player that determines years of service, salary, and other terms is a contract. Crosby's contract with the Penguins is for $104.4 million over 12 years.

draft (draft) Professional teams scout and select new players to join their roster in the draft. Crosby was chosen first in the 2005 NHL Draft.

junior hockey (JOON-yur HAH-kee) Junior hockey is a level of hockey for players ages 16–20. Crosby played junior hockey for the Rimouski Océanic.

points (points) In hockey, points are the combined number of goals and assists for a player. Crosby led the NHL in points in the 2006–07 and 2013–14 seasons.

rivals (RYE-vulz) Two opponents that are particularly competitive against each other are rivals. The U.S. and Canadian national hockey teams are rivals.

rookie (RUK-ee) A player in his or her first year in a new league is a rookie. Sidney Crosby was a star rookie for the Pittsburgh Penguins.

TO LEARN MORE

BOOKS

Buker, Rick. *100 Things Penguins Fans Should Know & Do Before They Die.* Chicago: Triumph Books, 2011.

Buker, Rick. *Total Penguins: The Definitive Encyclopedia of the Pittsburgh Penguins.* Chicago: Triumph Books, 2010.

Jordan, Christopher. *We Are the Goal Scorers: The Top Point Leaders of the NHL.* Toronto/New York: Fenn/Tundra, 2013.

WEB SITES

Visit our Web site for links about Sidney Crosby:
childsworld.com/links

Note to Parents, Teachers, and Librarians: We routinely verify our Web links to make sure they are safe and active sites. So encourage your readers to check them out!

INDEX

assists, 6, 8, 10, 12, 20
Canada, 4, 6, 8, 16, 20
captain, 4, 10, 12, 14
draft, 8, 10

goals, 6, 8, 10, 12, 18, 20
injuries, 4, 14, 19
Olympics, 4, 16, 18

playoffs, 12, 18, 19
points, 10, 12, 20
Stanley Cup, 4, 14, 18, 20

RECEIVED SEP 2 9 2015